# Henri Nouwen

FINDING OUR *Sacred* CENTER

A journey to inner peace

TWENTY THIRD 23rd
PUBLICATIONS
NEW LONDON, CT 06320
WWW.23RDPUBLICATIONS.COM

**Second printing 2012**

TWENTY-THIRD PUBLICATIONS
A Division of Bayard
One Montauk Avenue, Suite 200
New London, CT 06320
(860) 437-3012; (800) 321-0411
www.23rdpublications.com

ISBN 978-1-58595-847-4

Printed in the U.S.A.

Library of Congress Cataloging-in-Publication Data

Nouwen, Henri J. M.
     Finding our sacred center : a journey to inner peace.
       p. cm.
     ISBN 978-1-58595-847-4 (hardcover)
   1. Nouwen, Henri J. M.—Diaries. 2. Spiritual life—Catholic Church.
I. Title.
     BX4705.N87A3 2011
     248.4'82—dc23

                                 2011034978

PHOTO CREDITS: Regina Tours (5, 12, 31); Julie Rattey (6, 19, 22, 44);
Kerry Weber (10, 35); Tom P. Galvin, www.tompgalvin.com (25)

Published in Canada by Novalis

| | |
|---|---|
| Publishing Office | Head Office |
| 10 Lower Spadina Avenue, Suite 400 | 4475 Frontenac Street |
| Toronto, Ontario, Canada | Montréal, Québec, Canada |
| M5V 2Z2 | H2H 2S2 |
| www.novalis.ca | |

ISBN 978-2-89646-440-1

Cataloging in Publication is available from Library and Archives Canada.

We acknowledge the financial support of the Government of Canada
through the Canada Book Fund for business development activities.

For more information about
Henri Nouwen, his work, and the
work of the Henri Nouwen Society,
visit **www.HenriNouwen.org**.

# Contents

# *Melannie Svoboda, SND*

It was January 1990, the dawn of a new decade. Henri Nouwen, world-renowned spiritual writer, was in France writing. And he was struggling—again. His writing wasn't going well. His mind "was in cramps." Frustrated and discouraged, he decided to go to Lourdes, even though it was the "off-season," to give his "anxious heart a rest." This short journal is the result of his three-day stay.

The journal is typical Nouwen, that is, it is personal, simple, and profoundly inspiring. Nouwen hooks his ruminations on the major symbols he encounters at Lourdes: the water, a large stone, the grotto, and the basilica. At each turn, he reflects on what he is experiencing in his own heart, and, while doing so, he carries us along with him. Throughout his stay, he strikes up conversations with ordinary people—something he was very good at doing: the smiling man who sells him souvenirs, the woman in the coffee shop who insists on heating up his pastry, and the taxi driver who takes him back to the train station.

Though short, this journal contains many spiritual gems. Nouwen writes, "...the only way for me to see the world is through (Jesus') eyes." He speaks tenderly of Mary, "my gentle counselor," and says, "In her, God interrupted history and started to make everything new." While reflecting on the huge, round stone at the end of the Stations of the Cross, he muses, "The resurrection of Jesus simplifies everything."

Lourdes restores Nouwen's inner peace
and helps him return to his "sacred center."
He realizes, of course, that he does not
need to be at Lourdes to find peace and
joy. The purity, simplicity, and freedom he
experiences at Lourdes "belong to the heart
and can be lived anywhere." His worries and
fears for the future are assuaged at Lourdes.
He says simply, "Nothing can be predicted.
Yet all is already held safe in the divine
embrace that holds me still."

Whether we have been to Lourdes or not
does not matter. Whether we are a Nouwen
"fan" or we have never heard of him is beside
the point. This small journal is bound to
touch our own restless and searching hearts
and help us to find again our own sacred
center, the living Christ within us.

# "I love people.

I love them if they believe in God or not. I'm not out to convert everybody. That's not my attitude. A lot of people contact me who have absolutely no sense of God, who I love deeply, who love me deeply. So I'm not saying that if you don't believe in God you're not a good person. It's just the opposite. Some of the best people are often people who have no formal religious interest, and a lot of religious people are very narrow-minded and extremely anxious. These lines are hard to draw, but I do believe that you continue to see people searching for the Spirit, searching for something that transcends the earth."

HENRI NOUWEN, 1992

# INTRODUCTION

Henri Nouwen was a searcher. Born in Holland in 1932, he was ordained a Catholic priest in 1957, but was not nearly satisfied that his education was complete. He studied psychology, taught at Notre Dame, Yale, and Harvard, tasted the monastic life among the Trappist monks, lived among the poor in Latin America, and finally found his home at L'Arche Daybreak, a Canadian community dedicated to providing homes for the intellectually and physically disabled.

At L'Arche he found people who did not know he was famous and did not care. At L'Arche he found patience and tolerance and calm. But, although finally rooted, Henri continued to wander, never quite at home with himself.

Henri was a writer, and writers are never satisfied, never still—if they become so, they will no longer write. Henri wrote. Every day, Henri wrote. And Henri wandered. And in January of 1990, just after the turn of the new decade, Henri wandered to Lourdes.

Much has been made of Henri Nouwen's weaknesses and vulnerabilities. But one of his greatest strengths is illustrated in his words above. Henri was able to love everyone. Henri was able to understand and to deeply, firmly, totally connect with the knowledge that Hindu or Christian, Muslim or Jew, atheist or acolyte, we are all of us linked, all of us vital, all of us beloved— equally and without distinction.

There can be no argument that Henri Nouwen was profoundly Christian. In *Henri Nouwen: His Life and Vision*, Michael

O'Laughlin wrote that Henri was "almost uniquely able to make connections to Jesus as part of whatever he was then talking about." Yet Henri never saw Christianity as an impediment to accepting people of other faiths—to deeply and sincerely respecting their differing beliefs. He was so completely rooted in his own faith that he was never threatened by the fact that others might glimpse God through a different window.

Nor did it matter that others might find his Christian faith unfathomable. Henri knew what he knew. In an age where Christianity might sometimes seem unfashionable, where some might find themselves embarrassed or even apologetic to admit to being Christian, Henri was unabashedly, overtly, obviously Christian. Henri knew what he knew.

And in January of 1990, Henri knew he had to go to Lourdes. What follows is what he wrote of his journey. It was off-season. Lourdes was empty but tangibly fulfilling. Henri will walk you down the rain-soaked streets. He will take you along with him to a quiet café; to pray in the basilica; and ultimately to explore the Stations of the Cross.

This was a pivotal time for Henri. He had not yet written his last, great books and struggled to give them form...to find meaning in his life's work. Listen to how Mother Teresa's profound and simple wisdom guided his hands and his heart. And whether you travel to Lourdes in the flesh or only through the pages of this little book, know what Henri knew—that you are not alone.

KATHRYN SMITH
*Administrator*
*The Henri Nouwen Legacy Trust*

# Not Berlin, but Lourdes

Today is January 7, 1990, and I am in Lourdes. A few weeks ago I felt convinced I should go to Berlin to experience the radical changes taking place in Europe at the beginning of a new decade. I didn't go. I am not completely sure why not, but when I gave careful attention to my inner voice, I knew that I had

to stay away from large crowds, noisy debates, and great political movements. The next decade is one that will change radically the face of our planet. The question for me was: How to live that decade?

The answer came quickly: in deep communion with Jesus. Jesus has to be and to become evermore the center of my life. It is not enough that Jesus is my teacher, my guide, my source of inspiration. It is not even enough that he is my companion on the journey, my friend, and my brother. Jesus must become the heart of my heart, the fire of my life, the lover of my soul, the bridegroom of my spirit. He must become my only thought, my only concern, my only desire. The thousands of people, events, ideas, and plans that occupy my inner life must become all one in the one and only name: Jesus.

I know that I have to move from speaking about Jesus to letting him speak within me, from thinking about Jesus to letting him think within me, from acting for and with Jesus to letting him act through me. I know the only way for me to see the world is to see it through his eyes. Everything has to become very simple, very unified, very focused. It is no longer a question of being up to date or well-informed. At this moment in history—my own as well as that of the world—I have to go to the very center of being: the center where time touches eternity, where earth and heaven meet, where God's Word becomes human flesh, where death and immortality embrace. There is really no longer a question of options. With an unmistakable clarity, I have heard a voice saying, "Give me everything, and I will give you everything."

And so, I didn't go to Berlin. Instead, I went from my temporary base at L'Arche in Trosly to Compiègne, from Compiègne to Paris, and from there to Lourdes.

*I know the only way for me to see the world is to see it through Jesus' eyes*

There are very few pilgrims at this time of the year. I am here alone. After the long, tiring night on the train, I arrived at "the little convent" of the Sisters of the Immaculate Conception at 7:30 a.m. I slept, went to the grotto where Mary appeared

to Bernadette,
celebrated the
Eucharist of the
Epiphany in the
basilica, and prayed.

Why am I here?
To give my life to
Jesus. To make Jesus
the very center of
my existence. But
how is this to come
about? Mary is here
to show me; Mary is
here to be my gentle
counselor, to take
me by the hand and
let me enter into full
communion with her
son.

I am afraid, but Mary is here and tells me to trust. I realize that I can make Jesus the heart of my heart only when I ask Mary to show me how. She is the mother of Jesus. In her, God interrupted history and started to make everything new. And so I too have to put myself under her protection as I seek to enter the '90s with Jesus alone.

As I live these days, I want to stay away from all the big news on TV and radio. For just a while, I want to fast from political, economic, and religious debates. I simply want to be very close to her who spoke to Bernadette in the grotto. I trust that she will open my heart for a new encounter with Jesus.

# The Water

A CALL TO PURITY

Today, a dark and rainy day, is the feast of the
Baptism of Jesus. At the grotto, everything
speaks of water: the rushing Gave River, the
drizzling rain from the cloudy sky, the spring
of Masabielle. There are few pilgrims. The
large space before the grotto is empty. Here

and there I see people with their umbrellas walking close to the place where Mary spoke to Bernadette. They touch the rocks forming the cave, watch the little spring, let their rosaries move through their fingers, look up to the statue of Mary, make the sign of the cross, and light a candle. It is gray, cold, damp, and empty. No music, no songs, no processions.

I want to be purified. I want to be cleansed. I go to the baths. There, two men instruct me to undress. They wrap a blue apron around my waist, ask me to concentrate on what intercessions I want to ask of Mary, then lead me into the bath and immerse me in the ice-cold water. When I stand again, they pray the Hail Mary with me and give me a cup of water from the spring to drink. There are no towels with which to dry myself. And so, still shivering and wet, I put my clothes back on, go back to the grotto, and pray. Looking up at the statue, I read the words, "I am the Immaculate Conception," and I understand. The people of Israel were led through the Red Sea; Jesus was baptized in the Jordan; someone poured water over my head shortly after I was born. Blessed are the pure of heart; they shall see God.

I am looking. I am listening. Do I see and hear? I want to, but I cannot force myself. Bernadette saw a young woman dressed in white and blue. She saw her smile, she heard her voice. On this dark, rainy day there is little to please the senses: no sun, no foliage, no candlelight. Under little tin-roofed stalls, some men are burning candles in bunches of hundreds, but it doesn't warm my heart.

Everything comes back to the basic questions: "Do you want to see? Do you want to let go of your sin? Do you want to repent?" I do, I do, but I do not know how to make it happen.

I walk from the grotto to the basilica above it. Many steps lead me to the little square overlooking the valley of the Gave. Entering the crypt of the church where the Blessed Sacrament is adored during the day, I see the host enclosed in a large glass triangle held up by a tree-like structure. A few people are praying. It is very quiet. I sit down before the altar on which the Blessed Sacrament rests.

After an hour, I sense a deep need for forgiveness and healing. I go to a priest in the chapel of confessions across the way from the basilica. He speaks to me for a long time. His French is difficult for me to understand. I strain to listen. He mentions the poverty of Lourdes in January and says, "It is good for you to be here now. Pray to Mary and Bernadette, and be willing to let go of the old and let God's grace touch you as it touched Mary and Bernadette. Don't be afraid to be poor, alone, naked, stripped of all your familiar ways of doing things. God is not finished with you yet." I listen, and I know he speaks in Jesus' name. He absolves me of all my sins and tells me to say a prayer that reminds me that I belong to God. I shake hands with this stranger-friend, and I feel a little lighter.

Evening is approaching. I walk along the promenade where, during the summer, thousands of people—young and old, sick and healthy—pray and sing. No one is there now.

Leaving the grounds of the grotto, I enter a coffee shop attached to a souvenir store. I

# Don't be afraid to be poor, alone, naked, stripped of all your familiar ways of doing things

used to hate Lourdes "kitsch": the plastic madonnas and plastic Bernadettes in all sizes and styles. But today I don't have that feeling. I buy two little statues for a handicapped woman who knew I was coming to Lourdes. She had lost her phosphorescent madonna and asked me to buy her a new one. To be sure, I buy two. The man who sells them to me is all smiles. I sit down in the coffee shop and order a cappuccino with a pastry. The woman tells me the pastry will taste better when hot. She heats it for me and asks me how I like it. I am the only one in the shop. I stay for an hour reading a book.

At 6 p.m. I pass the grotto again. I pray for a while. A man in a plastic coat is sweeping away the water and arranging the candles. A few people sit in the grotto praying their rosaries. It is very quiet. The floodlight has been turned on to mark the cave, the statue, and the altar in the cave.

It is dark and still raining when I leave to go back to "the little convent." I hold my rosary in my hands and say the Hail Mary with a loud voice as I walk home. Only the barren trees along the Gave can hear me. My whole being prays for purity: purity of mind, purity of heart, purity of body. I remember the prayer my mother taught me: "By your Immaculate Conception, O Mary, purify my body and sanctify my soul." I say it again and feel a little bit of peace touching me from within.

# The Stone

## A CALL TO SIMPLICITY

The next morning as I leave "the little convent," it is soft outside. Here and there behind the clouds I see a few patches of blue sky. The rain has stopped. Before my leaving for Lourdes, my friend Mirella told me to be sure to make the Stations of the Cross. These are life-size representations of fourteen moments in the Passion of Jesus placed along a small path, beside a winding road leading me to

19

the top of a tree-covered hill. To encourage me, Mirella had given me a little book with reflections on the Stations by Thomas Philippe, OP. With the booklet in my hands, I enter the park where the Stations are placed. I am alone.

After a few minutes' walk, I arrive at the first Station: "Jesus is condemned to death."

*Who is innocent in front of the innocent One?*

Looking up, I see a long stairway leading up to a bronze statue of Jesus staring down at me. Around him stand a group of fierce Roman soldiers. A multilingual sign reads: "Please go up the stairs on your knees." I do, even though there are large puddles of water on the steps. As I crawl to the top and come closer to the statue of Jesus facing me,

I get a deep sense of being like Peter. The figure of a small boy carrying a bowl and towel reminds me of Pilate's washing his hands in front of the crowds and declaring his innocence. Who is innocent in front of the innocent One? Who does not participate in his condemnation? As I come so close to the statue that I can touch it, I see that many visitors have written their names on Jesus' cloak. What were they trying to express? At one place I read: Joan, Michael, Francine, and Ron. What went through the minds of these people when they marked the image of Jesus with their names?

As I walk up the hill, I see Jesus falling three times; I witness his encounters with Mary, Simon of Cyrene, Veronica, and the weeping women. I see Jesus robbed of his clothes, nailed to the cross, and dying between two criminals. And I stand in front of the Pietà: Mary holding the dead body of Jesus in her lap. Then the road takes me down again to the bottom of the hill. There I spy a great cave and, in front of it, eleven statues circling the body of Jesus before it is laid in the tomb. I stand there for a long time reading Thomas Philippe's reflection about the last Station. He writes about the

tomb of my life where I must bury my old self. He says:

> The Christian life is a continual struggle against the old self. Not just a struggle in the sense of a battle, but a real putting in the tomb....All authentic Christian lives... know these long "tunnels" where one does not see anything anymore, where one understands nothing, where one is disgusted. Jesus makes us descend with him in the tomb, in the weakness, in the darkness, in everything that seems dead in our heart, but always to rectify us, to purify us, to liberate us.

As I look into the long, deep, dark cave in the rock and see the body of Jesus carried into that darkness, I want to enter with him and let all my selfish needs and desires, all my violence, resentments, lusts, and petty jealousies be put there, never to be taken up again. I pray for hope, for courage, and, most of all, for trust that the darkness is simply a tunnel and not a final destination. It seems such an endless struggle, and I often wonder if I will ever see the end of this dark passage.

As I walk away from the last Station expecting to find the exit from the park, I turn a corner and suddenly see a huge, round stone. From its center many rays are carved, reaching out to its far edges. It looks like the sun; it speaks of light and freedom. Its simplicity stops me in my tracks. There are no statues, no gestures, no movements. Just a great, round, free-standing boulder. Beside it are the words: "At the first sign of dawn… they found that the stone had been rolled away." Turning to the other side of the stone, I read: "He has risen, as he said he would."

An immense solitude and peace come over me. I am quite alone: no people, no statues,

no events to think about. Just that huge
stone. All the Stations of the Passion, so full
of drama and tragedy, seem to be gone. All
that remains is this very quiet place—empty,
simple, pure, and unpretentious. I had
not expected this "fifteenth Station." It's
not really a Station. It's more like a gentle
reminder, a moment of hope, a small
rearrangement of nature. It does not demand

my attention as did the life-size figures of
the Stations. I can pass it by and let it go
unnoticed. But something is happening
within me—a leaping up.

I have often made the Stations of the Cross,
in many places and circumstances, but here
I stand, surprised by a joy I didn't expect to
come to me at the end of this long walk. It is
the utter simplicity of it all that touches me
most. The resurrection of Jesus simplifies
everything. Life is so complex. There are
so, so many memories, so many events, so
many possibilities. There are people to pay
attention to, events to reflect on, choices to
ponder. And there is the ongoing question
of priorities: who to respond to first, what to
consider first, where to go first....But here,
before the rolled-away stone, a simple center
from which hope radiates, all is very simple. I
sense the deep truth of this simplicity. Jesus

is risen. All has become one. The emptiness of the place makes me realize that I don't have to go anywhere, meet anyone, do anything. All is here, now, in this instant.

Gone are all those emotions felt while crawling up the steps and looking at the condemned Jesus. Gone too are all feelings of guilt and shame. Gone as well are all the questions about what to do in the years ahead.

The risen Jesus is not bound to any place or person. He is totally free. Simplicity and freedom belong together. Purity too. I realize that I need not be at Lourdes to find peace and joy. Lourdes simply reminds me that purity, simplicity, and freedom belong to the heart and can be lived anywhere.

Mary met Jesus after the resurrection, but not as he was met by Mary of Magdala or

John or Peter or the disciples on the road to Emmaus. She didn't need to be convinced of anything. Her heart was so simple, so pure, so free that her encounter with her risen son could be completely interior. A heart that truly knows Jesus doesn't need an apparition. Jesus and Mary were always present to each other in sorrow and joy. I know now that the purer and simpler my heart is, the more clearly I will see— wherever I am.

*I know now that the purer and simpler my heart is, the more clearly I will see —wherever I am*

I leave the park. Cars rush by. I walk to the town and buy lunch in the same coffee shop I visited yesterday. The lady is happy to see me again and serves me with special kindness. A young man writes in his notebook while eating his lunch. When I ask him where he is from, he says, "From Brazil." I feel an urge to find out more about him, but something tells me it is better to remain silent, enfold him in my prayer, and walk back to the grotto.

# The Grotto
## A CALL TO INNOCENCE

After three days in Lourdes, I know it is time to go home. When I came I had thought about staying a week, maybe even two weeks. But as I prayed at the grotto, in the crypt, and on the hill of the Stations of the Cross, it became very clear that staying more than three days would not be good. I have received all I could expect to receive. The time for asking has passed. Now I have to live the life I am so clearly called to live: simple, pure, free.

Last night I sat in front of the grotto holding a large candle in my hands. It would take more than a day for the candle to burn down, but I wanted to be, for a while, with the flame that would pray all through the night.

I prayed for all the people who surround me close by, as well as for those far away. As I looked at the statue of Mary in the niche above the grotto, I lifted up to her not only all those who are part of my family, my community, my circle of friends, but all the people whose lives will go through so many changes in the coming decade. Ten years from now, the world will be so different. How will it look? Will there be peace? Will there be less hunger and starvation, less persecution and torture, less homelessness and AIDS? Will there be more unity, more love, more faith? I have no

*I have to live the life I am so clearly called to live: simple, pure, free*

answers to these questions. I know nothing of the future. I don't have to. But I pray for all the people who will journey with me over the next decade and ask Mary to keep them all close to her son.

A taxi brings me to the railroad station. The driver tells me there are 420 hotels in Lourdes and that every year between Easter and the first of November, close to five million pilgrims come to the grotto to pray to Mary. With a smile he says, "You are not in that number, you come out of season."

It takes from 8:30 in the morning until 4:30 in the afternoon to travel from Lourdes to Paris. As I sit in the train, I let the landscape slip by. My thoughts are of Mary, Bernadette, and the ten years ahead of me. The word that comes to mind is "innocent." Mary was innocent. Her soul wasn't wounded by sin.

That is why she could offer a perfect place to the child of God. Her innocence was an innocence from which the Word of God could take flesh and become the lamb to take away the sin of the world. Her innocence made her become the Mother of Sorrows because she who had no sin sensed more deeply the sins of humanity for which her son came to suffer and die.

I think of Bernadette. She was only fourteen when she saw the "Lady." Everything I have read and heard about her makes me aware of how simple and clear-headed she was. She would be the last to desire an apparition and, when she saw the Lady at the grotto, she remained quite aloof in the midst of all the confusion that followed. She stated what she saw and heard—no more, no less—and stuck to it, no matter what people said of her or did to her. She possessed a true innocence:

simple, straightforward, clear-minded,
unaffected by the sensational responses
in her surroundings. Bernadette wanted
nothing for herself, but only to mediate the
message of the Lady. She must have been
a very strong person, free from the usual
manipulations of people. Her innocence
was that of a child who knows she is loved
and trusts her own sense of what is good

and worthy. It was with her innocence that Bernadette could see and hear the mother of Jesus and be a simple, unambiguous witness to her words about prayer and penance.

The train goes fast. After Bordeaux, it stops only at Tours before arriving at Paris. I talk to two women in the dining car. They don't know each other, but both are connected with the French diplomatic corps and have traveled widely: Argentina, Nigeria, Lebanon, the Emirates, Niger, Germany, Switzerland, and so on. I see a lot of suffering in their faces, but I see also a simple human goodness underlying all the disillusionments of an ever-changing life. I keep thinking of innocence, and I sense that beyond all my own darkness, there is innocence too. Like Mary and Bernadette and these two traveling women, I too carry God's innocence in me. Before I am sinful, I am innocent; before

I participate in the evil of the world, I am touched with goodness. I realize after my days in Lourdes that I have to claim that innocence in me. It belongs to my deepest self. It is given to me by God my Creator; it is reclaimed for me by Jesus my Redeemer. It is this innocence that makes me hear the voice that says, "You are my Son, my beloved; on you my favor rests" (Luke 3:22).

I know that I am called to live at the place of innocence: the place where Jesus chose to live. There he made his home and asks me to make mine. In that place I am loved and well held. There I do not have to be afraid. And from there I can forgive and heal and make things new.

The countryside between Tours and Paris is peaceful: many green fields, here and there touched by a few rays of sun breaking through the clouds. Can I live innocently on this planet in the years ahead? Can I choose to make my innocence my home, think from there, speak from there, act from there? It is a hard choice because my insecure self wants so much to be part of a world that controls, rewards, and tells me whether I am good or bad. But I can go beyond that insecurity and discover my sacred center, fashioned in secret and molded in the depths of the earth.

I know that every time I choose for my innocence, I don't have to worry about the next ten years. I can simply be where I

*I realize after my days in Lourdes that I have to claim that innocence in me*

am, listening, seeing, touching in the very moment, always sure that I am not alone but with him who called me to live as God's child. Jesus prays to his Father for his disciples, saying: "I do not ask that you take them out of the world but that you keep them from the evil one. They do not belong to the world any more than I belong to the world. Consecrate them in the truth" (John 17:15–17). My innocence is hidden in God. As a child who belongs to God, I can claim my innocence without leaving the world. In fact, as an innocent one, I am sent into the world: "As you sent me into the world, so I have sent them into the world" (John 17:18).

Within a few minutes I will arrive in Paris, at the Austerlitz station. It is the city of saints and sinners, Jerusalem and Babylon, a constant invitation to prayer and a constant bombardment of the senses. It is the city of Notre Dame and the Place du Pompidou, the city of hidden holiness and spectacular exhibitions. I have to walk through it as the innocent one and trust that I will touch the innocence of my companions in life. I have to trust that whenever I speak from the place of innocence, my words will heal; that whenever I act from the place of innocence, my actions will bring forth life, in Paris or anywhere else.

For the innocent ones there is nothing to fear. They will see God wherever they are. Blessed are the pure of heart. Blessings on Paris. Blessings on the world. Blessings on all of its people.

CONCLUSION

# The Call of the Bridegroom

I am back home again. I find letters on my table and little notes about people who tried to call me. It all looks quite ordinary. A few friends express surprise that I didn't stay longer: "I thought you were going for a week. Why back so soon?" I tell them that I had received all I could hope for and wanted to return to my work. They nod understandingly, but I realize I have a hard time expressing what I feel. As I look out of my window, I see the familiar old chestnut trees and, behind them, the vague contours of the forest of Compiègne. I say to myself, "I must go back to work. But not back to the old way of working." When I left for Lourdes,

I felt anxious and tense. My writing wasn't going well. I was trying too hard, pushing too fast, wanting too much. It seemed as though my mind was in cramps. Everything I did was done so deliberately and self-consciously that nothing could flow freely. Every thought, idea, vision, or perspective seemed frozen. My inner movements had become spastic. I complained to my friends: "I feel so tense inside—no inspirations, no easy streams of good words, no spontaneity."

Then, suddenly, I left. Not to Berlin to be excited by visions of a new world, but to Lourdes to be alone and let my anxious heart rest. Now, five days later, I am sitting again at my desk. I remember Mother Teresa's words to me twelve years ago: "Write simply," she said, "very simply. People need simple words." I heard that same call again in Lourdes. It is so easy for me to get caught up in complicated thinking. It is hard to be simple because simplicity asks for a pure heart and an innocent eye, qualities that are gifts from God, freely given. I cannot just will them.

Much was given to me at Lourdes. Both Mary and Bernadette brought me close to the pure and innocent heart of Jesus. If there are any words to write, they will come from the Spirit of Jesus in me. I have to let the water of purification cleanse my many old ways of speaking and writing. My long-standing, "tried and true" patterns must be laid in the tomb. Trusting that the "right" words will be there when they *need* to be there.

*It is hard to be simple because simplicity asks for a pure heart and an innocent eye*

I feel less tense now, less anxious, less worried. It was good to be in Lourdes, good to "waste" time just being there among the saints. I have no great new plans, no big new ideas, no vision about the future, I have only the desire to remain close to that place in me where I can hear the voice that calls me "my son, my beloved," and that will tell me what to do, say, or write when the time for it

has come. The quiet grotto, the water from the well, the round sun-like stone are signs of hope calling me to remain always open to receive from Jesus the purity, simplicity, and innocence I desire. I am not alone. Jesus dwells within me. Whatever is pure, simple, and innocent in me comes from him. With his love I can love and give myself to others. With his eyes I can see God's face; with his ears I can hear God's voice; with his heart I can speak to God's heart.

I know that, alone, I cannot see, hear, or touch God in the world. But God in me, the living Christ in me, *can* see, hear, and touch God in the world, and all that is Christ's in me is fully my own. His simplicity, his purity, his innocence are my very own because they are truly given to me to be claimed as my most personal possessions. That is what Paul means when he says, "I have been crucified with Christ; yet I live, no longer I, but Christ lives in me" (Galatians 2:19–20). All the beauty of Mary comes from Jesus, yet she is so completely her own. All the sanctity of Bernadette is given to her by Jesus, yet she owns every part of herself with complete freedom. All that there is of love in me is a gift from Jesus, yet every gesture of love I am able to make will be recognized as uniquely mine. That's the paradox of grace. The fullest gift of grace brings with it the fullest gift of freedom. There is nothing good in me that does not come from God, through Christ, but all the good in me is uniquely my own. The deeper my intimacy with Jesus, the more complete is my freedom.

Whatever I am to be in the years ahead, anything that may be good about it comes from Jesus. But what comes from Jesus I can truly claim as most fully my own.

# The fullest gift of grace brings with it the fullest gift of freedom

❧

A little journey has come to its end. As I look up from my desk to the fog-covered trees of the forest of Compiègne, I realize that all I learned, I knew already. But all I learned was also new. My only hope was to make Jesus more fully the center of my life, the heart of my heart, the lover of my soul, the bridegroom of my spirit. He was always there, in a soft, gentle, hidden way. Yet he is there now as though he had never been there. He is always the same and never the same, always absent, always present, always searched for, always found. That's what God's love is about. The Lover and the Beloved are two and yet one, separated and yet in full communion, in anguish yet filled with ecstatic joy. Mary and Bernadette knew about this. In Lourdes I caught a glimpse of it again. A new decade has begun; nothing can be predicted. Yet all is already held safe in the divine embrace that holds me, too.

# Prayer for a New Day

O God,

Help us today to welcome Jesus in our lives,

The Jesus whom we meet in our own family,
   among our friends, and in our cities.

And truly believe that as we reach out,
   we will discover that Jesus is still
   among us...still smiles at us...and still
   gives us his blessing.

Bless us today...each one who listens to
   words of God.

And let something really new happen
   among us, that comes from your life-
   giving Spirit.

In this we pray.
   Amen.

HENRI J.M. NOUWEN

# About Henri Nouwen

The internationally renowned priest and author, respected professor and beloved pastor Henri Nouwen (pronounced Henry Now-win) wrote over forty books on the spiritual life. He corresponded regularly in English, Dutch, German, French, and Spanish with hundreds of friends and reached out to thousands through his eucharistic celebrations, lectures, and retreats. Since his death in 1996, ever-increasing numbers of readers, writers, teachers, and seekers have been guided by his literary legacy. Nouwen's books have sold over two million copies and been published in over twenty-two languages.

Born in Nijkerk, Holland, on January 24, 1932, Nouwen felt called to the priesthood at a very young age. He was ordained in 1957 as a diocesan priest and studied psychology at the Catholic University of Nijmegen. In 1964, he moved to the United States to study at the Menninger Clinic. He went on to teach at the University of Notre Dame, and the Divinity Schools of

Yale and Harvard. For several months during the 1970s, Nouwen lived and worked with the Trappist monks in the Abbey of the Genesee, and in the early 1980s he lived with the poor in Peru. In 1985, he was called to join L'Arche in Trosly, France, the first of over 100 communities founded by Jean Vanier where people with developmental disabilities live with assistants. A year later, Nouwen came to make his home at L'Arche Daybreak near Toronto, Canada. He died suddenly on September 21, 1996, in Holland and is buried in Richmond Hill, Ontario.

Nouwen believed that what is most personal is most universal; he wrote, "By giving words to these intimate experiences, I can make my life available to others." His spirit lives on in the work of the Henri Nouwen Society, Henri Nouwen Stichting, the Henri Nouwen Legacy Trust, the Henri J.M. Nouwen Archives and Research Collection, and in all who live the spiritual values of communion, community, and ministry, to which he dedicated his life.